DISS TO NORWICH

including Bressingham Steam Museum

Richard Adderson & Graham Kenworthy

Series editor Vic Mitchell

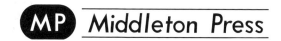

MP Middleton Press

Front cover: The photographer has taken advantage of a rare Winter's day of snow and cloudless skies to record no. 47581 Great Eastern *as it runs on to Trowse Swing Bridge with a down train on 5th January 1985. Trains are signalled over the bridge in both directions, an operating convenience impossible with the single-track bridge which replaced it. (S.McNae)*

Back cover (upper): See map caption opposite.

Back cover (lower): Looking very smart in its lined black livery, class B1 4-6-0 no. 61050 passes Norwich Thorpe Junction signal box as it steams away from the city with the 11.45am 'East Anglian' express for Liverpool Street on 10th November 1951. (R.Harrison)

> Readers of this book may be interested in the following society:
>
> *Great Eastern Railway Society,*
> *Ken Wheatley, Membership Secretary,*
> *69 Birchanger Lane,*
> *Birchanger,*
> *Bishops Stortford, CM23 5QA*

Published September 2018
First reprint January 2019

ISBN 978 1 910356 22 7

© Middleton Press, 2018

Production Editor & Cover design Deborah Esher
Design Cassandra Morgan

Published by
    Middleton Press
    Easebourne Lane
    Midhurst
    West Sussex
    GU29 9AZ
Tel: 01730 813169
Email: info@middletonpress.co.uk
www.middletonpress.co.uk

Printed and bound by CPI Group (UK) Ltd, Croydon, CR0 4YY

CONTENTS

INDEX

ACKNOWLEDGEMENTS

In addition to those individuals acknowledged in the photographic credits, we are most grateful to Geoff Ashton, Mike Bootman, Mike Rayner, Dave Taylor, and the family of Barry Mobbs, who worked at Diss station for nearly 30 years.

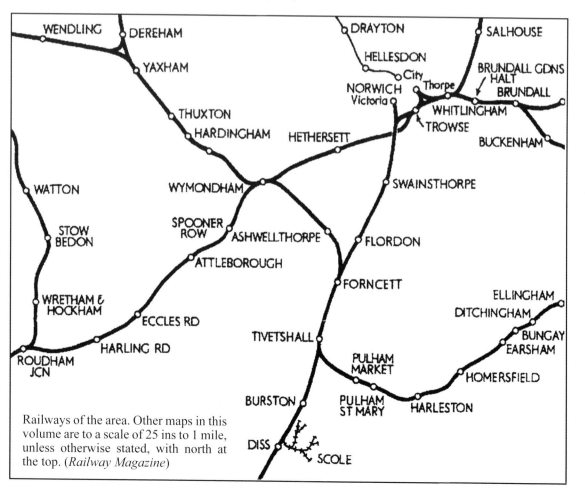

Railways of the area. Other maps in this volume are to a scale of 25 ins to 1 mile, unless otherwise stated, with north at the top. (*Railway Magazine*)

GEOGRAPHICAL SETTING

Diss to Norwich

Having crossed the River Waveney just to the south of Diss station, the route begins a gentle five mile climb with varying gradients to a two mile long level section where the underlying geology changes from chalk to crag. There is then a four mile descent, again with varying gradients to the valley of the River Tas. The undulating nature of the line continues with a summit less than two miles further north before the route crosses the River Yare on Lakenham Viaduct. The 1849 route to Victoria station remains virtually level while the line towards Thorpe station descends sharply for one mile to connect with that of 1845 from Cambridge and Ely.

Forncett to Wymondham

After its divergence from the route from Diss to Norwich, the branch fell quite sharply to cross the shallow valley of the River Tas, before a rather more gentle climb to its summit at Ashwellthorpe. The line then continued across undulating countryside to the junction at Wymondham.

HISTORICAL BACKGROUND

Diss to Norwich

Early in 1846, a second Ipswich & Bury Railway Act was passed for construction of what became the main line from the junction at Haughley to Norwich. The line from Haughley to Diss and Norwich opened in two stages during 1849; to Burston on 2nd July and onwards to Norwich Victoria on 12th December. When the line was opened there were three other routes already in existence terminating at Thorpe station, those from Ely, Yarmouth and Lowestoft. The link from Trowse Upper Junction to Trowse Lower Junction was brought into use on 8th September 1851.

The development north from Haughley was under the management of the Eastern Union Railway, one of the five companies which were amalgamated to form the Great Eastern Railway in 1862. The Act that brought about this change included a clause forbidding the GER from closing Victoria station, a situation which became increasingly uneconomic as time passed. Despite local opposition in the form of a well supported petition, agreement was finally reached with the Corporation to withdraw the remaining passenger services on 22nd May 1916, although the line from Trowse Upper Junction continued in use for goods traffic for a further 70 years.

On grouping, the Great Eastern Railway passed into the ownership of the London & North Eastern Railway on 1st January 1923, and the line became part of the Eastern Region of British Railways upon nationalisation on 1st January 1948.

After electrification north from Ipswich to Norwich, the full service from Liverpool Street to Norfolk's capital was introduced on 11th May 1987, although the section had been covered by the first electrically powered train just over a month earlier on 6th April.

After the changes which followed privatisation in the mid-1990s, services were provided by a succession of companies, using the brandings shown, as follows:

5th January 1997	'Anglia Railways'
1st April 2004	'one' (National Express)
27th February 2008	'National Express East Anglia' ('one' rebranded)
5th February 2012	'Greater Anglia' (Abellio)
January 2014	Rebranded 'Abellio Greater Anglia'
17th October 2016	Back to 2012 'Greater Anglia' but still with Abellio

Forncett to Wymondham

During the 1870s, a number of proposals for west to east lines across North Norfolk were seen by the Great Eastern Railway as threats to its monopoly. One of the perceived improvements that could be made was to provide an additional link from the south of the system to north and west Norfolk. This direct link from the former Eastern Union Railway main line to that of the Eastern Counties Railway would avoid the need for through traffic to reverse at Norwich and, after the opening of the south to west spur at Dereham, also give a direct route towards King's Lynn.

The Act for the new six mile route was passed in 1876 and the line opened in May 1881, passing to the London & North Eastern Railway on 1st January 1923. Closure to passengers took place on the outbreak of World War II in September 1939, with the service terminating on the 11th of that month. During the war, the line was used by a variety of freight services to provide materials for the large number of military facilities, which were based in Norfolk. In 1943, these materials included

"Petroleum Products in Rail Tank Cars" from the regional depot at Sandy Heath.

Closure to through traffic occurred in 1951, after which the remaining line towards Ashwellthorpe was served from the Wymondham end. After the end of its use serving A.King's scrapping facility, the connection was secured out of use and subsequently removed during 1976/77.

PASSENGER SERVICES

Diss to Norwich

In 1848, the Ipswich & Bury Railway ran five trains from Ipswich to Bury providing services for stations from Bramford to Stowmarket inclusive. When the line from Haughley to Norwich was opened in December 1849, a further three daily trains were provided, taking just over five hours to connect Norfolk's capital with London.

By August 1863, there were seven trains from Diss to Norwich, with varied calling patterns at the intermediate stations. Three of these served both Norwich Victoria and Norwich Thorpe, dividing at Trowse Upper Junction; each of the terminal stations also had two exclusive services.

These seven services were much the same into the early 1880s, but with a slightly different combination of Norwich termination points. North from Tivetshall, the service included two trains from Beccles to Victoria via the Waveney Valley route. A total of four trains called at Forncett, providing connections to the recently opened line to Wymondham.

By 1920, as a result of the complete closure of Victoria to passenger services in 1916, there were nine trains from Diss to Norwich Thorpe. In addition, there were four Norwich-bound Waveney Valley trains joining the main line at Tivetshall; three of these called at all stations with one stopping only at Trowse.

Little changed through the 1920s and 1930s, but, in the post-WWII years, a period of expansion of travel opportunities began. By 1950, there were 13 daily services provided, five of which called at all stations with the exception of Trowse, which closed on the outbreak of WWII. There were three further trains that called only at Tivetshall for Waveney Valley connections, and two more which arrived at Tivetshall from the Waveney Valley and then called at all stations to Norwich. There was a third service from the same source which called only at Forncett on its way to the County's capital.

The withdrawal of passenger trains from the Waveney Valley route in January 1953 and the closure of Swainsthorpe in July 1954 meant that, by the Summer of

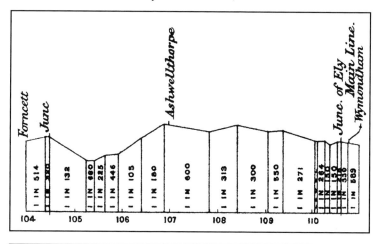

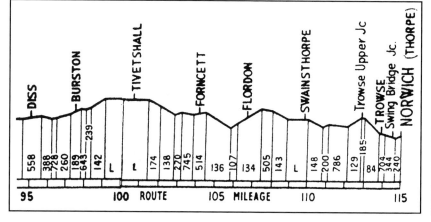

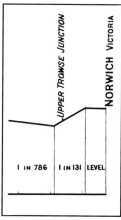

This is a dense railway timetable with columns for Miles, Fares (1st, 2nd, 3rd, gov class), station names ("Dow"), Week Days, and Sundays. Station stops listed include Bishopsgate Station, London, Mile End, Stratford, Forest Gate, Ilford (for Barking), Chadwell Heath, Romford, Brentwood, Ingatestone, Chelmsford, Witham Junction, Kelvedon, Marks Tey Junction, Colchester, Hythe, Wivenhoe, Ardleigh, Manningtree, Mistley, Bradfield, Wrabness, Dovercourt, Harwich, Bentley Junction, Capel, Raydon, Hadleigh, Ipswich, Westerfield, Bealings, Woodbridge, Melton, Wickham Market Junction, Marlesford, Parham, Framlingham, Saxmundham Junction, Leiston, Aldborough, Darsham, Halesworth, Brampton, Beccles Junction, Carlton Colville, Lowestoft, Aldeby, St. Olaves Junction, Haddiscoe, Reedham, Norwich, St. Olaves, Belton, Yarmouth, Bramford, Claydon, Needham, Stowmarket, Haughley Junction, Elmswell, Thurston, Bury, Finningham, Mellis, Diss, Burston, Tivetshall Junction, Pulham Market, Pulham Mary, Starston, Harleston, Redenhall, Wortwell, Homersfield, Earsham, Bungay, Ditchingham, Ellingham, Geldeston, Beccles, Forncett, Florden, Swainsthorpe, Norwich Victoria, Trowse, Norwich (Thorpe), Lowestoft, Yarmouth.

November 1865

The 1895 timetable to Ashwellthorpe can be found under picture no. 61.

1964, the timetable was rather less complicated. There was a total of 17 trains from Diss to Norwich, nine of which had originated at Liverpool Street and six at Ipswich; of the other two, one started from Stowmarket and one from Diss itself. Nine ran non-stop to Norwich, seven called at all stations and one stopped only at Tivetshall. The withdrawal of passenger services from the remaining intermediate stations took place on 7th November 1966.

Electrification in 1987 introduced a timetable in which 18 main line services, at broadly hourly intervals, ran from Diss to Norwich. The 2017/18 timetable listed no less than 37 main line trains leaving Diss for Norwich. Of these, 36 started at Liverpool Street, with just one, the first of the early morning originating at Ipswich.

Forncett to Wymondham

In 1882, the year after the line had opened, there were five daily trains, four of which called at Ashwellthorpe by request only. Four of the five services were timed to provide connections from the Ipswich direction; three of these four also connected with services from the Waveney Valley route, which had joined the main line at Tivetshall.

By 1920, the daily service had increased to six, all of which provided connections for main line services from the Ipswich direction, but with no convenient provision for the Waveney Valley trains. The last train of the day, the 8.05pm to Wymondham continued its journey via Dereham to Wells. The six daily trains were still provided at the time of closure in 1939.

LOWESTOFT, YARMOUTH, TIVETSHALL, and NORWICH.—Great Eastern.
Chief Traffic Man., Wm. C. May. Loco. Supt., A. J. Hill. Eng., H. Wilmer.

Down.	Week Days—Continued.																					
	aft	mrn	aft	mrn	mrn	mrn	aft	aft	aft	aft	aft	aft	aft	aft	aft	aft	aft	aft	aft	aft	aft	aft
LIVERPOOL ST. ..dep.				1059	1142	11 51	1230			1 0			1 30	1 42				2 15	3 10		3 22	
Stratford(West Ham) "				11 9		12 1								1 52				2 26				
Ilford "														2 1								
Romford "													1 52	2 11								
Harold Wood "				1130									2 0	2 19								
Brentwood & Warley "				1139		12 24							2 8	2 28								
Shenfield & Hutton. "				1145		12 31							2 14	2 36								
Ingatestone "				1152		12 38								2 43				2 54				
Chelmsford "				12 5	1228	12 50							2 29	2 54				3 3			4 [illegible]	
Hatfield Peverel				1215		1 0							2 39	3 4				3 13				
Witham 302, 306				1223		1 5							2 47	3 9				3 21				
Kelvedon † 339b				1231									2 55					3 29				
Mark's Tey 322				1241	1253								3 5					3 39				
Colchester ‡324 ... arr.				1250	1 2		1 36			2 8			3 14					3 48			4 33	
324 Clacton-on-Sea* arr					2 8		2 21			2 47								4 58			5 16	
Colchester ... dep.		1135		1254	1 7		1 39			2 11								3 53			4 36	4 42
Ardleigh				1 x3	1 16													4 2				4 51
Manningtree 325		1147		1 12	1 27													4 11				4 58
325 Harwich (P. Q.) arr.		12 5		1 58	1 58													4 42				5 20
325 " (Town) "		1212		2 5	2 5													4 49				5 27
Bentley 323		Stop		1 21	1 37													4 20				Stop
Ipswich 323 ... arr.				1 31	1 47		2 1			2 33							4 18	4 30	4 40		4 58	
Ipswich ... dep.	12 8			Stop	2 16		2 16		2 21	2 38	2 48					4 10			4 50		5 9	
Westerfield 323	1217								2 20		2 58					4 19					5 18	
323 Felixstowe (T) arr	1244				2 51		2 51			3 15									5 30		5 51	
Bealings	Stop								2 37		3 4					4 26					5 25	
Woodbridge									2 44		3 10					4 32					5 32	
Melton									2 48		3 14					4 36					5 36	
Wickham Market§315									2 59		3 25					4 47					5 47	
Saxmundham 322 arr.									3 9		3 34					4 57					5 57	
322 Aldeburgh .. arr.									3 41		4 6										6 28	
Saxmundham ... dep.									3 12		3 37										6 0	
Darsham, for Yoxford.									3 22		3 47										6 10	
Halesworth 317									3 36		3 58										6 24	
Brampton									3 45		4 7										6 33	
Beccles 320, 323 .. arr.									3 54	3 33	4 16								5 45		6 42	
320 Lowestoft (C.) arr				aft					4 23	3 56	4 41								6 10		7 14	
Beccles ... dep.				1 35					3 57	3 36	4 19								5 49	6 0	6 47	
Aldeby				1 44					4 6		4 28									6 9	6 56	
Haddiscoe 328				1 48					4 10		4 32									6 13	7 0	
328 Norwich (Th.) .. arr.				4 4																	8 35	
St. Olaves				1 54					4 16		4 38									6 19	7 6	
Belton ... [360, 363				2 0					4 24		4 47									6 27	7 15	
Yarmouth (Sth Tn) arr.				2 9					4 33	4 0	4 56								6 14	6 36	7 24	
361 Gorleston-on-Sea "		non		Stop						4 22												
Ipswich ... dep.		12 4	1230				2 6	2 18							4 5		4 24		4 45		5 3	
Bramford		1210						2 24							4 11							
Claydon		1215						2 29							4 16							
Needham		1223	1243					2 37							4 24						5 16	
Stowmarket		1231	1252					2 46							[illegible]		4 41				5 25	
Haughley 314, 318		1238	1258					2 58							5 10						5 33	
314 Bury St. Edmnds arr.			1 22					3 28									5 6					
Finningham		1247						3 7													5 42	
Mellis 304		1255						3 15													5 51	
Diss		1 2						3 23													5 59	
Burston	aft	1 8		aft				3 29														aft
Tivetshall 323	1259	1 16		2 22				3 38				4 8										6 47
323 Beccles ... arr.		2 39						5 32														
Forncett 308	1 6	1 24		2 29				3 46				4 15									6 15	6 54
Flordon		1 30						3 52				4 21										7 0
Swainsthorpe		1 36						3 58				4 27										7 6
Norwich (Vic.) 363 arr.		1 51						4 13														
Trowse ... [325	1 22	1 49		2 45				4 11				4 37									6 31	7 15
Norwich (Thorpe) 316 arr	1 26	1 53		2 49			3 5	4 15				4 42							5 44		6 35	7 19
316 Cromer ... arr.		3e18					4 4												6 49		7 38	9 6
316 Sheringham ... "							4 18												7 3			

Wednesdays only. — Luncheon Cars, London to Ipswich. — Sats. only. Luncheon Cars, London to Cromer. — Saturdays only. — Except Saturdays. Luncheon Cars to Yarmouth. — Saturdays only. Luncheon Cars to Yarmouth. — Saturdays only. — Saturdays only. — Except Saturdays. — Tuesdays only. — From Harwich and Parkeston to Ely, Doncaster, and York, see pages 325 and 314.

August 1915

FORNCETT and WYMONDHAM

Miles	Down.	Week Days only.						
		mrn	mrn	mrn		aft	aft	aft
	856 London (L'pool St.) dep.	5 0	5 30	10 3	..	1225	3 40	5 16
—	Forncett ... dep.	815	1020	12 49	..	3 31	6 32	7 55
3	Ashwellthorpe ... [883	821	1026	12 55	..	3 37	6 39	8 1
6¼	Wymondham 860, 862, arr.	828	1033	1 2	..	3 44	6 46	8 8

Miles	Up.	Week Days only.						
		mrn	mrn	aft	aft	aft	aft	
	Wymondham ... dep.	7 18	9 23	12 5	3 10	4 50	7 8	..
3¼	Ashwellthorpe ... [883	7 25	9 30	1212	3 17	4 57	7 15	..
6¼	Forncett 856, 858 ... arr.	7 31	9 36	1218	3 25	5 3	7 21	..
110¼	858 London (L'pool St.) arr.	1023	2 A 0	4 57	6 32	9S15	1138	..

A Arr. 1 20 aft. on Sats. E or E Except Sats. S or S Sats. only.

December 1938

1. Bressingham Steam Museum

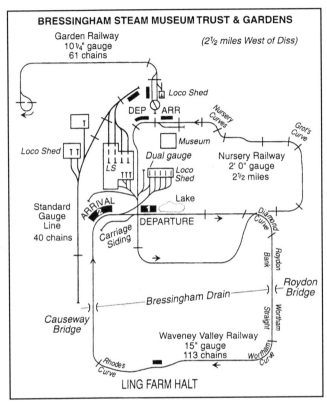

BRESSINGHAM STEAM MUSEUM TRUST & GARDENS

Garden Railway
10¼" gauge
61 chains

(2½ miles West of Diss)

Loco Shed

DEP ○ ARR

Nursery Curves

Grot's Curve

Loco Shed

Museum

Dual gauge

LS

Loco Shed

Nursery Railway
2' 0" gauge
2½ miles

Arrival

Lake

Standard Gauge Line
40 chains

Carriage Siding

DEPARTURE

Diamond Curve

Bank

Roydon

Roydon Bridge

Bressingham Drain

Causeway Bridge

Straight

Wortham

Waveney Valley Railway
15" gauge
113 chains

Wortham Curve

Rhodes Curve

LING FARM HALT

Route diagram for 2006.
(©TRACKatlas)

1. The Bressingham Steam Museum is located approximately three miles west of Diss station on the north bank of the River Waveney. From the early 1960s onwards, visitors to the nursery and gardens at Bressingham Hall would have found a growing collection of steam traction engines, but it was not until the middle of that decade that the location welcomed a railway track. The first line to be built was the Garden Railway, a 9½ inch gauge track tucked away at the edge of the site and often operated by *Princess*, a diminutive pacific which is seen in action on 21st June 1970. Some 25 years later, the railway was relaid to 10¼ inch gauge and partially rerouted, as seen in picture 10. (B.Harrison)

2. The Nursery line was built in time for the 1966 season, with a track gauge of 2ft 0in. During the late 1960s we see *Gwynedd* making its way round the 1½ mile circuit, with the museum's guiding force, Alan Bloom, enjoying his pipe on the footplate. *Gwynedd* was built as long ago as 1883 and spent its working life at Penrhyn slate quarry in North Wales before moving to Bressingham in 1966. (B.Adams)

3. The site gained a much higher profile with the arrival of a number of standard gauge locomotives from 1968 onwards. One of the first to arrive was Britannia class 4-6-2 no. 70013 *Oliver Cromwell*, fresh from hauling the 'Fifteen Guinea Special' marking the end of main line steam on BR on 11th August that year. Just seven days later it made a remarkable sight on a low-loader taking it from Diss station to its new home. (W.J.Naunton)

4. On the previous day 4-4-2T no. 80 *Thundersley* had made the same journey, thus achieving the distinction of being the first standard gauge locomotive to be seen here. The two locomotives attract plenty of attention as they stand outside the exhibition shed during the Winter of 1968/69. (W.J.Naunton)

5. Two engines are being prepared for a day's work on the Nursery Line around 1970. The somewhat ungainly looking machine in the foreground is the 0-6-0 well tank *Bronllwyd*, built by Hudswell Clarke in 1930, which had also worked at Penrhyn Slate Quarries before coming to Norfolk and receiving a complete rebuild in the late 1960s. It was to remain here for some 35 years before moving on to pastures new. (B.Adams)

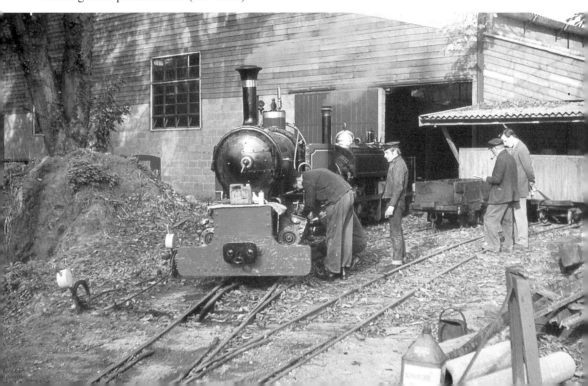

6. During the early 1970s, further main line express engines arrived in the shape of 4-6-0 no. 6100 *Royal Scot* and 4-6-2 no. 6233 *Duchess of Sutherland*, rescued from static display at Butlins Holiday Camps at Skegness and Ayr respectively. The two LMSR locos are seen here on 4th June 1972, in company with one of the traction engines from the collection. (R.J.Adderson)

7. Over the years, the attractions have included several locomotives from overseas. No. 141R 73, a 2-8-0 built in America for service in France, stands outside the shed on 28th August 1980, while *Peer Gynt*, a German-built 2-10-0 which spent its working life in Norway, is offering footplate rides. (R.J.Adderson)

8. *Mannertreu*, a 15 inch gauge pacific, makes its way through the woods along the Waveney Valley Railway, which had been open for some two years when this picture was taken on 22nd June 1975. This engine, together with sister locomotive *Rosenkavalier*, was built in Dusseldorf in 1937, and arrived at Bressingham in 1973. In 2018, both of them had been out of use for some years, requiring overhauls. (B.Harrison)

9. After the two pacifics were taken out of service, *St Christopher* became the mainstay of services on the Waveney Valley Railway. This 2-6-2T engine was built in 2001 and first appeared here in 2011. Complying with the notice, it waits to head off along the grassgrown tracks on its 1½ mile trip through the countryside on 30th May 2014. (R.J.Adderson)

↑ 10. The terminus for the rebuilt Garden Railway was far more visible to visitors than the previous one had been. A brand new locomotive was built at Bressingham for the line, and was named *Alan Bloom*, after the founder of the museum. The carriages are beginning to fill up as the engine waits to set off on another trip round the gardens on 30th June 2011.
(R.J.Adderson)

11. As the railway preservation movement prospered, the big engines were gradually moved away and nos 70013, 6233 and 6100 have all hauled main line trains again in the 21st century. In 2018, the only remaining standard gauge locomotives were static exhibits, with the exception of *Martello*, a former LBSCR "Terrier" tank engine. However, the three narrow gauge lines remained major tourist attractions as exemplified by this young lad who is enthralled by the sight of *Alan Bloom* being turned at the Garden Railway terminus.
(R.J.Adderson)

2. Diss to Forncett

DISS

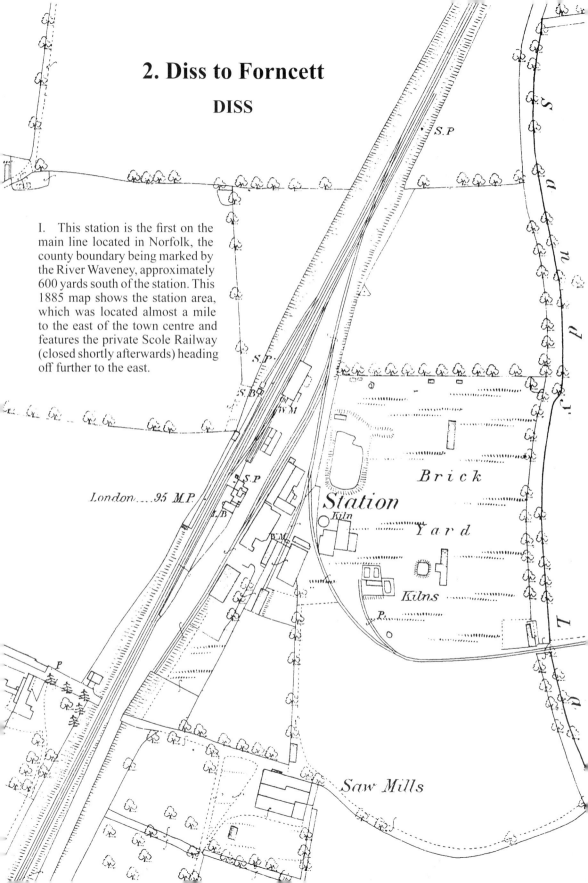

I. This station is the first on the main line located in Norfolk, the county boundary being marked by the River Waveney, approximately 600 yards south of the station. This 1885 map shows the station area, which was located almost a mile to the east of the town centre and features the private Scole Railway (closed shortly afterwards) heading off further to the east.

London ... 95 M.P.

Brick

Station

Yard

Kiln

Kilns

Saw Mills

12. Moving from tourist railways to the busy main line, our earliest picture here shows the signal box as it was in the 1920s. The small repeater arm towards the base of the signal post is noteworthy – this was provided to enable the signalman and train crews to confirm the aspect of the signal, as the main arm would be obscured from certain angles. (G.Austin coll.)

13. During the early 1950s, Britannia 4-6-2 no. 70012 *John of Gaunt* speeds towards the station with the 5.45pm train from Norwich, the up 'Norfolkman', which would call only at Ipswich on the journey to Liverpool Street. Class K3 2-6-0 no. 61957 stands next to the goods shed with a stopping passenger train, which has been shunted out of the way to enable the express to pass. The Summer timetable for 1952 shows that the local train left Norwich at 5.17 pm, and called at all stations except Swainsthorpe before arriving at Diss at 5.57 pm. Here it had to wait for some 28 minutes before resuming its journey to Ipswich. (I.C.Allen, Transport Treasury)

14. A member of the station staff poses with a mobile display publicising the Eastern Region modernisation plan of the 1950s, which promises 'Cleaner, more comfortable and faster travel'. An image of the prototype 'Deltic' locomotive features prominently, but these locomotives were confined to the East Coast main line, and the Great Eastern lines had to put up with considerably less powerful machines. (H.Chamberlain coll.)

For other views of Diss see Middleton Press album, *Ipswich to Diss*.

DISS (Norfolk).

POPULATION 3,164.
Distance from station, ½ mile.
A telegraph station.
HOTEL.—King's Head.
MARKET DAY.—Friday. FAIR.—November 8.
The church was built by the Fitzwalters. Skelton (the witty poet laureate to Harry the Bluff) was rector. In the vicinity is *Shimpling*, the Duke of Grafton's seat.
Passing BURSTON station, we arrive at TIVETSHALL JUNCTION, a telegraph station.

From *Bradshaw's Guide*, dated 1866.

15. We are looking south towards the slightly staggered platforms of the station somewhere around 1960. The goods shed is to the left of the picture, with the cattle pens and end loading dock between it and the main buildings on the up side, while there is just a brick-built waiting room on the down platform, visible beyond the signal box. (R.J.Adderson coll.)

16. Shunting in the goods yard was performed by horses until the late 1950s. 'Airborne', on the left, and 'Mary' take a break from their duties to pose for the photographer with two members of the station staff. (British Railways)

17. The yard sees unprecedented activity on the morning of 17th August 1968 as *Thundersley* is carefully winched onto a low-loader for the road journey to Bressingham, while *Oliver Cromwell* awaits its turn. Wagons in the yard provide evidence of three regular flows of goods traffic – fuel, grain and rotavators. The latter were built at Harleston, and this traffic had been handled at the station there for a few years prior to the closure of the western section of the Waveney Valley line in 1966. (R.J.Adderson)

18. After the horses left the scene, a road vehicle took over shunting duties, and this yellow painted John Deere tractor was to be found parked in the goods yard on 10th April 1984. The strong plates at each end align with the buffers on the railway wagons, and the coiled length of rope was no doubt used for towing purposes. It carries the registration number DDN 464K, revealing that it was registered in Leeds during the period 1st August 1971 to 31st July 1972. Grain traffic continued to use the yard until the late 1980s, and this tractor was noted there as late as January 1991. (R.J.Adderson)

19. There is a relaxed and unhurried air about the place as no. 47457 makes the station stop on a sunny Saturday morning. It is 9th June 1984, and the train is the 7.15am from Liverpool Street. (B.Harrison)

20. No. 90015 *Colchester Castle* runs into the station with a train for Liverpool Street on 23rd April 2009. The locomotive is in the livery applied during the period when National Express East Anglia held the franchise for running these services. Over to the right, a track machine is stabled in one of the two remaining sidings of the former goods yard. (R.J.Adderson)

21. During the build-up to electrification, both platforms were extended southwards in order to accommodate 10-coach trains. The extent of the lengthened platforms is seen here as no. 90004 *City of Chelmsford* propels a Norwich-bound train away from the station stop on 15th April 2015. Little shelter is available for passengers in inclement weather conditions. (R.J.Adderson)

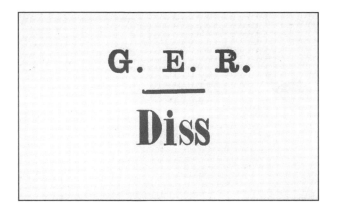

G. E. R.
————
Diss

22. Exceptionally heavy rain overnight on Sunday/Monday 15th/16th September 1968 led to the destruction of bridge no. 317, just over one mile north of Diss station. Fortunately, the damage was observed by a nearby farmer who contacted the local British Rail office, leading to prompt closure of the line before any trains were involved. A temporary bridge was installed quickly and services resumed on 4th October, but it was not until 2nd June 1969 that the permanent replacement bridge was completed. No. D1565 heads one of the first trains over the temporary structure. (G.L.Kenworthy coll.)

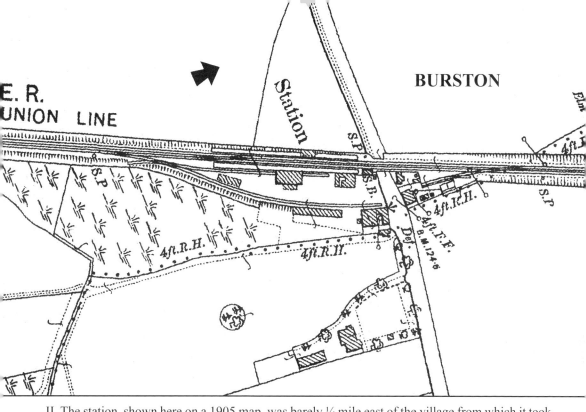

II. The station, shown here on a 1905 map, was barely ¼ mile east of the village from which it took its name. The population of the village was less than 500, leading to the very basic rail facilities depicted. Shimpling village, a similar distance to the east of the station, did little to add to the requirements with its population of just over 200. Of note is the cattle dock served by a short siding to the north of the level crossing, separate from the goods yard.

23. An up goods train stands at the platform in Great Eastern Railway days. The substantial wooden fencing on both platforms is noteworthy, while the goods shed obscures the main station buildings to the right of the picture. A small waiting shelter and brick-built urinal stand on the down platform – the shelter remained seemingly unchanged until closure, but the other facility disappeared during the intervening years. The rather ornate telegraph pole is worthy of note. (G.L.Kenworthy coll.)

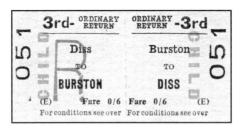

24. This was never one of the Great Eastern's showpiece stations and the station was looking extremely run down by the time this picture was taken in the early 1920s. (G.Austin coll.)

G. E. R.

From _____

TO

BURSTON

25. Provision of a replacement building was an early priority for the newly-formed LNER, and here we see the brand-new structure externally complete. These new facilities had been completed by 1928. (G.Austin coll.)

26. This is the public approach to the station, taken on the same day with the same smartly-attired gentleman adding human interest to the scene. The building was still standing in 2018, and was the major surviving feature of the stations between Diss and Trowse. (G.Austin coll.)

27. Class B1 4-6-0 no. 61253 runs through the station with a varied selection of vehicles in tow in August 1959. The configuration of headlamps on the engine indicates that this is an empty stock working. (G.Smith/Transport Treasury)

28. We are looking northwards from a departing train, shortly before passenger services were withdrawn on 7th November 1966. By now, the goods shed has been demolished, the absence of railings on the east side of the up platform showing where it had been, and the sidings are no longer in use, goods facilities having been withdrawn from 13th July 1964. (B.D.J. Walsh/GERS)

29. No. D206 drifts over the level crossing with the 6.08pm stopping train from Norwich to Diss on 27th June 1964. Only the fourth coach provides passenger accommodation, the other three being full brakes. It was unusual to see this type of engine on what was, on the face of it, a purely local service. However, the onward journey was quite complex and is worth recording. From Diss, the four vehicles continued to Ipswich, where the passenger coach was detached and milk tanks originating at Halesworth were added. Further vans were added at Colchester and Witham, and the milk tanks were detached at Ilford, before the train eventually terminated at Stratford. The three full brakes seen in the photograph then returned to Norwich as part of the next day's 2.45am newspaper and parcels train from Liverpool Street. (R.J.Adderson)

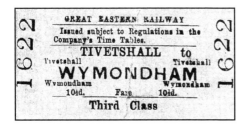

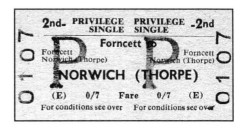

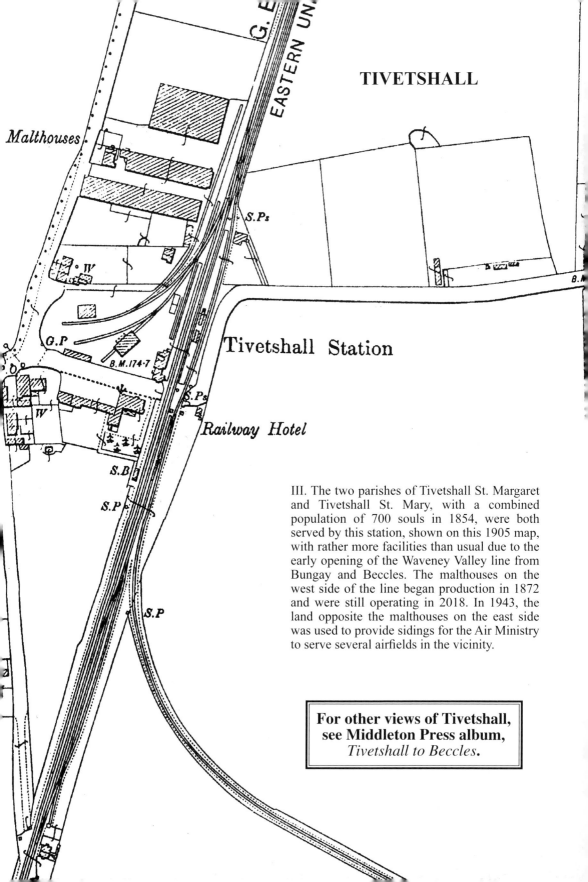

TIVETSHALL

Malthouses

S.Ps

W

G.P

B.M.174·7

Tivetshall Station

S.Ps

Railway Hotel

S.B

S.P

S.P

III. The two parishes of Tivetshall St. Margaret and Tivetshall St. Mary, with a combined population of 700 souls in 1854, were both served by this station, shown on this 1905 map, with rather more facilities than usual due to the early opening of the Waveney Valley line from Bungay and Beccles. The malthouses on the west side of the line began production in 1872 and were still operating in 2018. In 1943, the land opposite the malthouses on the east side was used to provide sidings for the Air Ministry to serve several airfields in the vicinity.

For other views of Tivetshall, see Middleton Press album, *Tivetshall to Beccles*.

30. This view looking northwards gives a good overall view of the station as it was early in the 20th century – the postcard bears an August 1909 postmark. The six people on the up platform appear to be uniformed railway staff, while those on the other side of the line are probably waiting passengers. As was typical in such scenes, all ten are looking at the photographer, rather than the approaching train. Half a mile or so behind the photographer were the water troughs which had been installed in 1896 at a cost of £2923 and were removed in 1945. (Bill King coll.)

31. Now we are standing at the north end of the up platform, looking towards Diss, sometime around 1959. This platform is an island, with the outer face being used by Waveney Valley line trains, and no doubt the fairly substantial waiting room on this platform was provided for passengers awaiting branch line connections. The main buildings are concentrated at the south end of the shorter up platform, while the goods yard and shed are squeezed into a somewhat cramped area behind the platform. (R.J.Adderson coll.)

32. At much the same time, a Brush type 2 diesel locomotive shunts on the loop line past the island platform. Engines of this class first appeared in the area in 1957 and very soon found themselves on all kinds of trains, ranging from main line expresses to branch line goods workings. The signals are a contrast with the modern motive power, being of GER origin. Over to the left, the water tower fed the three water cranes at the station, while a separate facility on the east side of the line further south met the needs of the water troughs. (N.Smith)

33. Our next four pictures illustrate the scene as it was in the mid-1960s, not long before passenger services ceased. Here a DMU from Norwich passes the Watneys Maltings as it runs into the station on a stopping service to Ipswich. The 1966 timetable shows that the intermediate village stations were served by eight down and nine up trains immediately prior to closure. (B.D.J.Walsh/GERS)

34. No. D1770 speeds through the station with an up express. This type of locomotive first appeared at Norwich in 1965, and they soon became first choice for the London expresses, a role which they fulfilled until electrification in 1987. The engine is in the original two-tone green livery, the coaches are maroon and the station sign has a blue background: all colour schemes which would vanish within a few years with the introduction of the corporate British Rail image. (B.D.J.Walsh/GERS)

35. It is interesting to compare this picture of the station building, taken from the road, with that of nearby Flordon (picture 59). The buildings are strikingly similar, but it appears that some rebuilding has taken place here over the years. Two patches of lighter brickwork around the doors testify to the changes, whilst the Flordon picture gives some idea of the original design. (B.D.J.Walsh/GERS)

36. The traditional level crossing gates were replaced by a new design of gates from 7th February 1965. These were known as Boom Gates and were still fairly new when this picture was taken. Tivetshall seemed to be a favourite place for experimental level crossing arrangements, as Hales Street crossing, just to the south, had acquired remotely-controlled lifting barriers in 1959 – the first in the country, according to a local newspaper. (G.L.Kenworthy coll.)

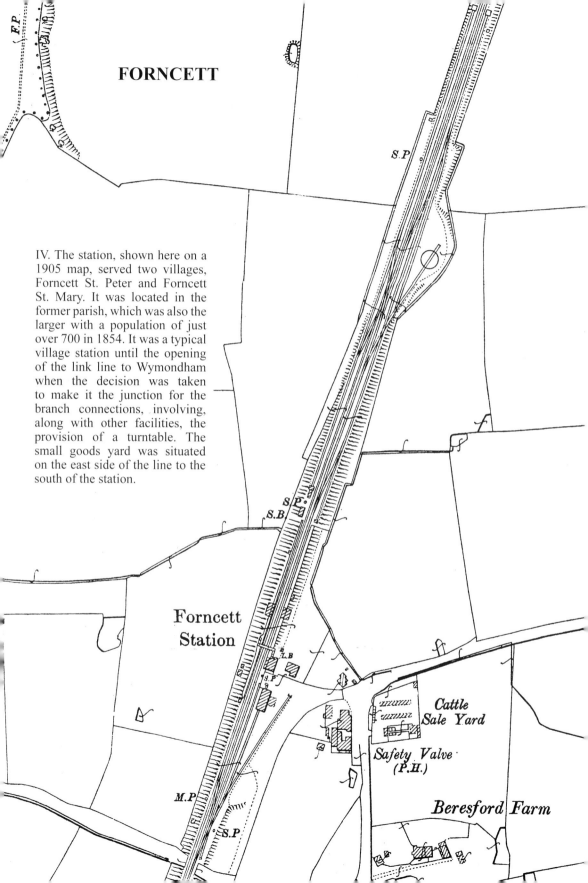

FORNCETT

IV. The station, shown here on a 1905 map, served two villages, Forncett St. Peter and Forncett St. Mary. It was located in the former parish, which was also the larger with a population of just over 700 in 1854. It was a typical village station until the opening of the link line to Wymondham when the decision was taken to make it the junction for the branch connections, involving, along with other facilities, the provision of a turntable. The small goods yard was situated on the east side of the line to the south of the station.

Forncett
Station

Cattle
Sale Yard

Safety Valve
(P.H.)

Beresford Farm

37. Our first look at this location dates from 7th October 1911, and is looking southwards with the station in the mid-distance. The siding to the west of the main running lines terminates at a very substantial bufferstop, seemingly constructed of timber and old rails, which protected the signal box and grounded coach body from over-vigorous shunting, while that on the east provides an inspection pit. (GERS/Windwood coll.)

38. We now move to the down starter signal for a closer view of the station on the same day. Both platforms have timbered surfaces, and the shelters are also of wooden construction. The two-storey station master's house, built at a lower level, emerges from the trees behind the up platform. Goods traffic ceased on 28th December 1964. (GERS/Windwood coll.)

39. This picture, dating from the inter-war years, provides a good view of the booking office, again of largely wooden construction, and the footbridge, which remained virtually unaltered until passenger services were withdrawn on 7th November 1966. By this time, the platforms had been renewed. (Stations UK)

40. We are looking northwards along the rain swept platforms around 1960, with the gentlemen's toilet block standing some distance away from the up platform buildings. Over on the down platform, the section of the waiting shelter with the canopy is that which appeared in our 1911 pictures, and a matching extension has been added at the north end. Even at this late date, the sign on the door to the southern part of the building specified 'Ladies Waiting Room', with the northern part being simply 'Waiting Room'. (R.J.Adderson coll.)

41. In later years the wooden buildings on the up platform were replaced by this somewhat functional office, seen here on another wet day not long before the closure. Standing on an embankment, this station could be a very exposed place, and indeed it suffered substantial wind damage during a storm in 1908. (RCTS Archive)

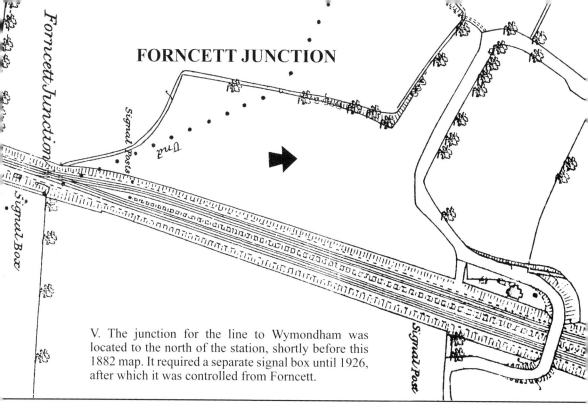

FORNCETT JUNCTION

Forncett Junction

Signal Posts

Signal Box

Signal Post

V. The junction for the line to Wymondham was located to the north of the station, shortly before this 1882 map. It required a separate signal box until 1926, after which it was controlled from Forncett.

42. Looking northwards from the down starter signal at Forncett, we see quite a complex track layout, with the boundary fence describing a large semi-circle to accommodate the 44ft 9ins turntable. A GER tank locomotive stands on the up refuge siding with two 6-wheel coaches forming the Wymondham train on 7th October 1911. The junction is just visible beneath the arch bridge in the distance. (GERS/Windwood coll.)

43. Wymondham branch trains ran on the main lines for approximately 28 chains between the station and the junction. This view is taken immediately north of the bridge referred to in picture 42; Forncett Junction signal box is to the right and the tracks to Wymondham make a sharp bend as they head away from the main line, again on 7th October 1911.
(GERS/Windwood coll.)

44. North of the junction, the lines to Wymondham and Norwich ran parallel for some distance before the branch headed away to the west. Here we are looking north towards the divergence on 1st December 1984. The trackbed of the branch is still visible and running at a slightly lower level, which is emphasised by the heights of the arches of the distant bridge. This bridge, and the one on which the photographer is standing, were built in conjunction with the Wymondham line, and followed the numerical sequence applicable to the branch. A class 31 locomotive heads towards Norwich in the Winter sunshine. (D.C.Pearce)

3. Ashwellthorpe Branch

ASHWELLTHORPE

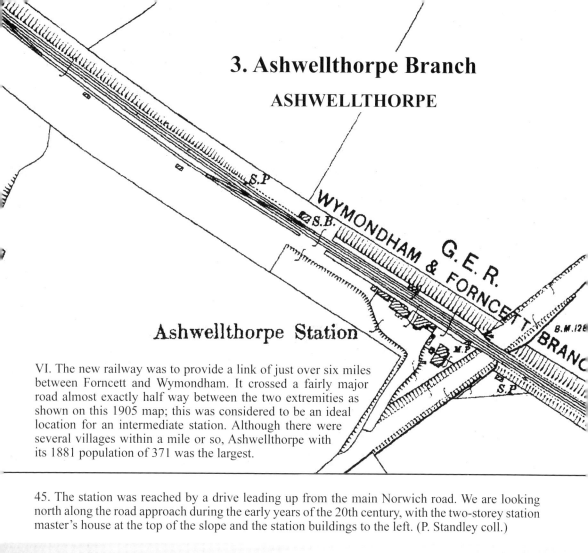

Ashwellthorpe Station

VI. The new railway was to provide a link of just over six miles between Forncett and Wymondham. It crossed a fairly major road almost exactly half way between the two extremities as shown on this 1905 map; this was considered to be an ideal location for an intermediate station. Although there were several villages within a mile or so, Ashwellthorpe with its 1881 population of 371 was the largest.

45. The station was reached by a drive leading up from the main Norwich road. We are looking north along the road approach during the early years of the 20th century, with the two-storey station master's house at the top of the slope and the station buildings to the left. (P. Standley coll.)

46. Here is a view looking westwards along the platforms when the station still handled passenger trains, probably during the 1930s. The main range of buildings are on the down platform, with just a simple shelter sufficing for travellers heading in the other direction. Goods traffic was withdrawn from 4th August 1951, and within 12 months the tracks here had been lifted. (Stations UK)

47. The station master's house and down platform buildings are easily recognisable in May 1966, by which time the site had been turned over to industrial use. Half a century later the structures were still there, albeit somewhat modified, while the rest of the site had developed into a linear industrial estate, which had eradicated all other traces of the former railway usage. (S.Moore)

48. After the line was closed as a through route, the tracks from Wymondham remained in place to a point some two miles west of Ashwellthorpe station. During the mid-1950s, the truncated line was one of several locations used in a British Transport Films production, an instructional film entitled 'The diesel train driver – dealing with faults'. A 2-car Derby DMU, not normally seen in the area, featured strongly, and here we see car E56018 with the film crew and BR staff during a break in filming. The main Norwich to Ely line runs in front of the buildings seen in the distance. (R.J.Adderson coll.)

49. During the 1950s this remaining section was sometimes used for storage of redundant rolling stock, and by 1962 a scrapyard had been established at the eastern end. As a result, the former running lines were, for much of the decade, filled with all kinds of coaching stock awaiting their fate. The normal procedure was for non-metallic materials to be removed here, usually by burning, leaving the metal underframes to be moved to King's scrapyard at Norwich for cutting up. One such coach underframe appears on the left of this general view of the scrapyard. (R.Harrison)

50. At the head of this row of coaches, seemingly abandoned in the heart of the countryside, are three electric power cars with vehicle M28586M leading. These dated back to 1930 and had spent their working lives on the Manchester to Altrincham service. Next come two bogie parcels vehicles, followed by five Pullman cars. The coaches dealt with here ranged from ancient wooden-bodied vehicles to modern Bulleid stock displaced by the Bournemouth electrification in 1967, and from suburban electric multiple units to the opulent Pullmans. (R.Harrison)

51. A 204 hp diesel shunter is busy with a long rake of coaches destined for the scrapyard. Again, former Southern Region Pullman cars are prominent. We are a short distance east of the junction, and the former double track remained in place from this point right up to the scrapyard. Both tracks here consist of bullhead rail mounted on concrete sleepers, but, by contrast, other stretches of the double track were still formed of rail sections dating back to the opening of the line. (I.C.Allen/Transport Treasury)

WYMONDHAM NORTH JUNCTION

52. The junction with the main line was controlled from Wymondham North signal box until November 1963, after which the points were worked from a two lever ground-frame. This arrangement lasted until 1976, when the branch, by then long reduced to the status of a siding, was recorded as out of use pending removal. Here is the junction in its final form, seen from a passing train, with just a trailing connection from the up main line. A map and an early illustration of this junction were included in our earlier volume *Ely to Norwich*. (B.D.J.Walsh/GERS)

4. Forncett to Norwich
NORTH OF FORNCETT

53. The night of 26th/27th August 1912 brought torrential rain to much of Norfolk, leading to widespread flooding across the county. As a result, the swollen waters of the River Tas swept away the three-arch railway bridge a mile or so south of Flordon station. This was the scene shortly afterwards, during the early stages of work to replace the bridge. The working conditions are somewhat primitive, and the two baulks of timber enabling workmen to make a precarious crossing of the river are noteworthy. Trains between Diss and Norwich were diverted via Ashwellthorpe and Wymondham until a new bridge was brought into use on 2nd October, just over five weeks after the storm. (Courtesy Norfolk County Council)

54. Not far from the rebuilt bridge, a plaque on the front of a house records the way in which the coming of the railway briefly boosted the activity in this quiet part of Norfolk. A limekiln had been flourishing by the early 1840s at Tharston, a short distance to the east of the subsequent route of the railway, and it was not surprising that a brick-kiln would follow after the discovery of suitable clay just below the surface. (G.L.Kenworthy)

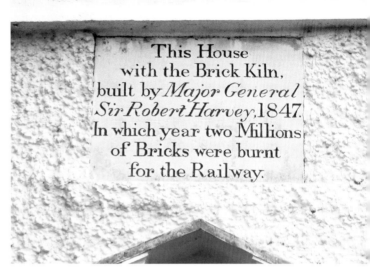

This House with the Brick Kiln, built by *Major General Sir Robert Harvey*, 1847. In which year two Millions of Bricks were burnt for the Railway.

Flordon Ballast Pit

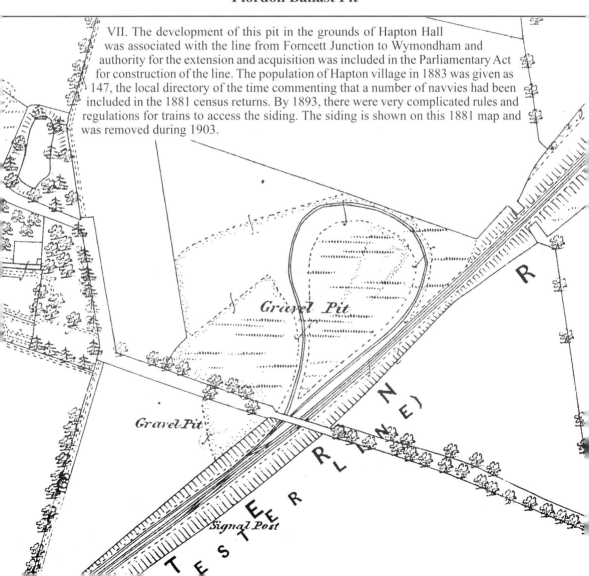

VII. The development of this pit in the grounds of Hapton Hall was associated with the line from Forncett Junction to Wymondham and authority for the extension and acquisition was included in the Parliamentary Act for construction of the line. The population of Hapton village in 1883 was given as 147, the local directory of the time commenting that a number of navvies had been included in the 1881 census returns. By 1893, there were very complicated rules and regulations for trains to access the siding. The siding is shown on this 1881 map and was removed during 1903.

Gravel Pit

Gravel Pit

Signal Post

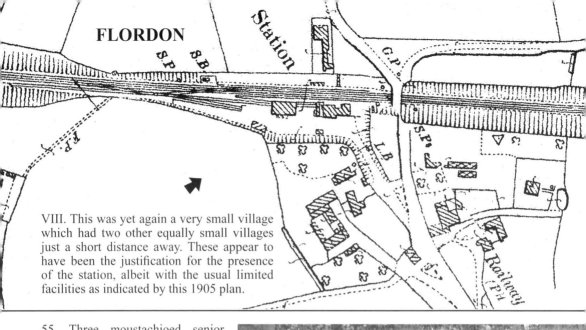

FLORDON

VIII. This was yet again a very small village which had two other equally small villages just a short distance away. These appear to have been the justification for the presence of the station, albeit with the usual limited facilities as indicated by this 1905 plan.

55. Three moustachioed senior railwayman keep company with their younger colleagues as members of the station staff pose for the photographer in front of a rather battered GER nameboard. This picture dates from the final years of the GER, as it bears a postmark date of September 1922.
(P.Standley coll.)

56. An up express hauled by a 'Britannia' class 4-6-2 emerges from under the road bridge on 9th December 1954. It is a commonplace scene, repeated several times each day and, apart from the photographer, there is nobody around to witness it.
(Stations UK)

57. Whatever the architectural merits of the building or the intricacies of the signalling and trackwork, it was very often the little details that brought stations to life, as exemplified in this short section of the up platform, photographed in May 1966. There are three blue enamel signs, two advising the station name, and the other an often welcome facility provided by the railway company. Three luggage trolleys are waiting for custom, although it is unlikely that they saw much use by this time. Colourful posters enliven the walls, with one advertising travel to the forthcoming World Cup, and another extolling the delights of travel in Germany – those who know their football history will appreciate the irony of these two posters appearing next to one another. (S. Moore)

58. The guard exchanges a few words with a member of the station staff - probably *the* member of the station staff - as a DMU pauses on its way to Norwich during the Summer before closure. The station is well-provided with totem signs, which would become sought-after collectors' items in the years to come. (B.D.J.Walsh/GERS)

59. It is April 1969, and perhaps surprisingly the door to the station building remains open, providing access to the disused platforms. Unlike that at Tivetshall (see picture 35) the building appears to have changed little over the years. (S.Moore)

60. A signal post provides a fine overall view of the station as it was in April 1969. Apart from the boarded-up signal box and redevelopment of the goods yard, which had closed on 19th April 1965, there is little to indicate that the last passenger train had called some 2½ years earlier. Even the signal box nameboard has avoided the attention of souvenir hunters. Everything seen here was subsequently demolished, and in 2018 there was very little to indicate that the station had ever existed. (S.Moore)

SOUTH OF SWAINSTHORPE

61. 'Britannia' class 4-6-2 no. 70006 *Robert Burns* approaches the rural Newton Greenways level crossing, roughly midway between Flordon and Swainsthorpe, on 14th March 1953. It is hauling the up 'East Anglian' on a 130 minute schedule from Norwich to Liverpool Street and the gleaming engine, less than two years old, makes a fine spectacle in the Spring sunshine. (R.Harrison)

NORWICH, TIVETSHALL, WYMONDHAM, DEREHAM, and WELLS.—Great Eastern.

Miles.	Fares 1 cl. s.d.	Fares 3 cl. s.d.	Return 1 cl. s.d.	Return 3 cl. s.d.	Down.	Week Days mrn	mrn	mrn	mrn	aft		aft	aft	aft	aft	aft	aft	aft	aft			Sundays aft		
					Thorpe Station, Norwich ....dep.	6 45	Mondays only.	8 25	1035	1247		3 20	4 7	....	5 22	6 15	7 5	....	8 12	....	....	7 0	....	....
1	0 2	0 1	0 3	0 1½	Trowse	6 50		8 30	1040	1252		3 25	4 12	....	5 27	6 20	7 10	....	8 17	....	....	7 6	....	....
6¾	1 2	0 4½	1 8	0 9	Hethersett	7 0		d	1050	1 2		3 35	....	....	5 37	6 30	....	....	8 27	....	....	7 16	....	....
10¼	1 8	0 7	2 6	1 2	Wymondham.arr	7 8		8 46	1059	1 11		3 44	....	....	5 46	6 39	7 25	....	8 36	....	....	7 25	....	....
—	....	....	....		182 London*.dep.	....		5b10	....	9 0	10 0	....	....	Tuesdays only.	Saturdays only.	3b20	....	5b0	....	....	....	....	....	....
—	....	....	....	....	Mls Tivetshall dp	....		8 0	1022	1232	1243	....	....			6a1	....	6 58	....	....	....	....	....	....
—	....	....	....	....	3½ Forncett.. "	....	7 22	8 26	1035	1243	1253	....	....			6 15	....	7 43	....	....	....	....	....	....
—	1 9	0 8	2 6	1 3	6¾ Ashwelthrpe	....	7 28	8 32	1041	1249	1259	....	....			6 21	....	7 49	....	....	....	....	....	....
—	....	....	....	....	10¼ Wymondhm	....	7 35	8 39	1048	1256	1 6	....	....			6 28	....	7 56	....	....	....	....	....	....
—	....	....	....	....	170 London*.dep.	....		....	5 45	9 10		1155	....			2 30	....	....	5 15	....	....	3 25	....	....
—	....	....	....	....	170 " (St.Pan.)"	....		....	....	9 15		12 3	....			2 35	....	....	5 8	....	....	....	....	....
—	....	....	....	....	Wymondham dep	7 11	* Liverpool Street. † St. Pancras.	8 48	11 1	1 13	Mons. and Sats.	3 49	....		5 47	6 44	7 26	7 57	8 30	....	....	7 28	....	....
14	2 3	0 9	3 3	1 6	Kimberley.......	7 18		....	11 8	1 20		3 56	....		5 54	6 51	....	....	8 47	....	....	7 36	....	....
15¾	2 7	0 11	3 8	1 10	Hardingham	7 23		8 58	1113	1 25		4 1	....		5 59	6 56	....	....	8 52	....	....	7 41	....	....
17½	2 11	1 0	4 2	2 0	Thuxton	7 27		....	1117	....		4 5	....		6 3	7 0	....	....	8 56	....	....	7 45	....	....
19¾	3 3	1 1	4 7	2 2	Yaxham	7 33		....	1123	1 34		4 12	....		6 10	7 6	....	f	9 2	....	....	7 52	....	....
21⅝	3 6	1 2½	5 0	2 5	Dereham 177 arr.	7 38		9 7	1128	1 39		4 17	4 44		6 15	7 11	7 44	8 14	9 7	....	....	7 57	....	....
					Dereham 177 dep.	7 40		9 9	1130	1 45		4 23	....	5 40	6 18	7 15	....	8 16	9 17	....	....	8 0	....	....
26½	3 9	1 6	5 6	2 9	North Elmham ..	7 49		9 18	1139	1 54		4 32	....	5 49	6 27	7 24	....	8 25	9 26	....	....	8 9	....	....
27¾	3 9	1 7½	5 11	3 0	County School ...	7 54		9 23	1144	1 59		4 37	....	5 54	6 33	7 29	....	8 30	9 31	....	....	8 14	....	....
31½	3 9	1 9	6 8	3 6	Ryburgh	8 1		9 30	1151	2 6		4 44	....	6 1	6 40	7 36	....	8 37	9 38	....	....	8 21	....	....
33¾	3 9	1 11	6 6	3 10	Fakenham	8 7		9 36	1157	2 15		4 50	....	6 6	6 48	7 43	....	8 43	9 45	....	....	8 27	....	....
38¾	4 8	2 4	7 11	4 8	Walsingham	....		9 47	12 8	2 26		5 1	....	....	7 0	7 53	....	8 54	9 56	....	....	8 38	....	....
43¼	5 8	2 8	9 2	5 3	Wells 177 ...arr.	....		10 0	1222	2 40		5 15	....	....	7 15	8 7	....	9 7	1010	....	....	8 52	....	....

a Wednesdays only from Tivetshall. b Via Forncett. c Stops on Tuesdays when required to set down. d Stops on Tuesdays when required to take up. e Stops to take up for London. f Stops on Mondays to set down. g Mondays and Saturdays. i Except Mondays and Saturdays. j Arrives at 12 31 aft. on Mondays and Saturdays. k Saturdays only.

December 1895

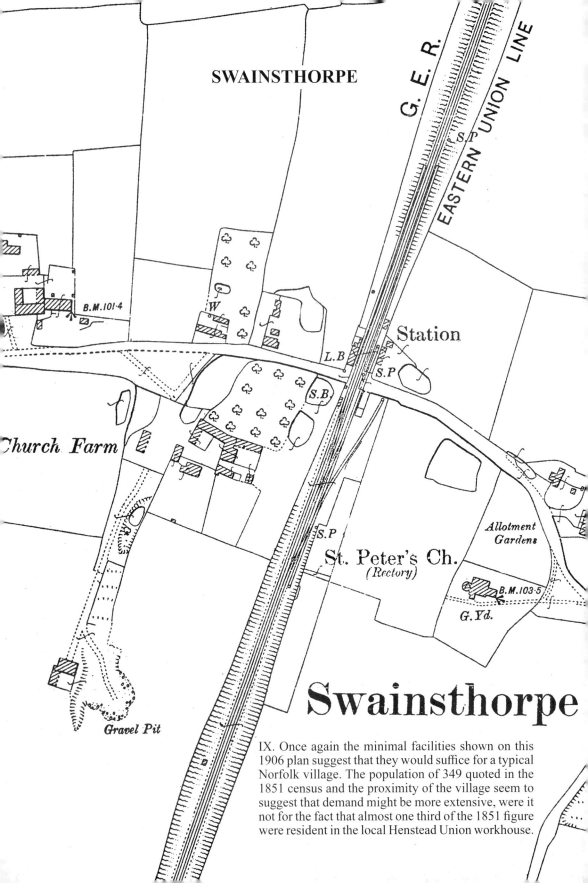

SWAINSTHORPE

G. E. R.

EASTERN UNION LINE

S.P

Station

S.P

B.M.101·4

W

L.B

S.B

Church Farm

S.P

St. Peter's Ch.
(Rectory)

Allotment
Gardens

B.M.103·5

G.Yd.

Gravel Pit

Swainsthorpe

IX. Once again the minimal facilities shown on this
1906 plan suggest that they would suffice for a typical
Norfolk village. The population of 349 quoted in the
1851 census and the proximity of the village seem to
suggest that demand might be more extensive, were it
not for the fact that almost one third of the 1851 figure
were resident in the local Henstead Union workhouse.

62. We are looking northwards along the tracks through the station, probably in the 1930s, with the track layout very much as shown on the map. The siding on the right is an interesting feature, running under the loading gauge, past the short cattle dock and through a gate across the road to terminate adjacent to some wooden sheds behind the up platform. (P.Standley coll.)

63. A single passenger is waiting patiently on a seat at the otherwise deserted station as we look southwards during the 1930s. The level crossing gates are open to road traffic, so he will have to wait a while for his train. Passenger services were withdrawn with effect from 5th July 1954, and goods traffic from 13th July 1964. (Stations UK)

64. Viewed from the railway side, the station building appears to be a fairly straightforward structure, albeit embellished with some fancy brickwork and extravagant chimneys. By 2nd April 1967, the siding across the road had vanished and a domestic garage fitted neatly into the space it once occupied. (S.Moore)

65. It was only from the west that the full extent of the three-storey building could be appreciated. Here is this revealing aspect, again on 2nd April 1967, some ten years before it was demolished. After that, just the toilet block remained, standing in splendid isolation for the use of the signalman. (S.Moore)

66. Overhead equipment for the impending electrification is already in place as no. 47544 accelerates an up train over the level crossing on 27th October 1985. The signal box remained in use for another 12 months and it was then moved to the northern terminus of the Wells & Walsingham Light Railway, where it was still to be seen in 2018. (R.J.Adderson)

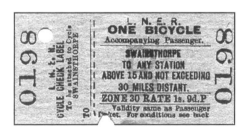

EXCURSION TRAIN:—

8.15 a.m. Swainsthorpe to Yarmouth (S.T.) and Lowestoft (Central), calling at Flordon, Forncett, Tivetshall, Pulham Market, Pulham St. Mary, Harleston, Homersfield, Earsham, Bungay, Ditchingham, Ellingham, Geldeston (Halt), and Beccles, returning from Yarmouth (S.T.) at 7.35 p.m., and Lowestoft (Central) at 7.20 p.m.

Swainsthorpe Excursion, August Bank Holiday - 7th August 1922.

TROWSE UPPER JUNCTION

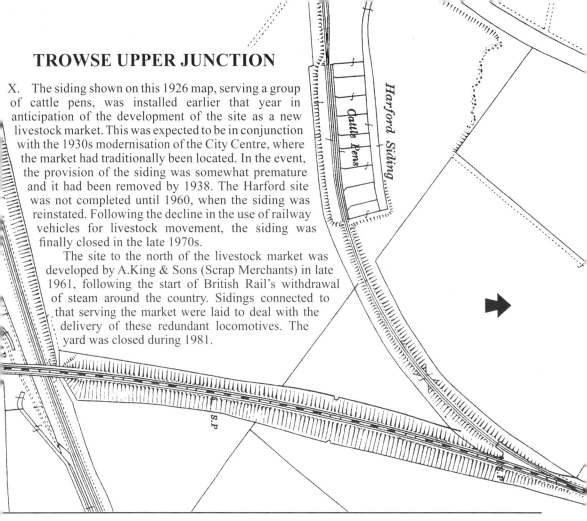

X. The siding shown on this 1926 map, serving a group of cattle pens, was installed earlier that year in anticipation of the development of the site as a new livestock market. This was expected to be in conjunction with the 1930s modernisation of the City Centre, where the market had traditionally been located. In the event, the provision of the siding was somewhat premature and it had been removed by 1938. The Harford site was not completed until 1960, when the siding was reinstated. Following the decline in the use of railway vehicles for livestock movement, the siding was finally closed in the late 1970s.

The site to the north of the livestock market was developed by A.King & Sons (Scrap Merchants) in late 1961, following the start of British Rail's withdrawal of steam around the country. Sidings connected to that serving the market were laid to deal with the delivery of these redundant locomotives. The yard was closed during 1981.

Harford Siding

Cattle Pens

S.P.S

67. Having negotiated Trowse Upper Junction, an up goods train approaches the viaduct during the 1950s, hauled by class J39 0-6-0 no. 64765. The bridge visible to the extreme left carries the short-lived Harford siding. (R.E.Vincent/Transport Treasury)

68. From time to time, the line to Victoria was used for shunting movements in association with single line working, as it was deemed safer to reverse trains on to the goods branch rather than over the sharply curved and steeply graded main line. On one such occasion, 13th March 1960, no. D5529 brings its train off the branch before setting off southwards on the "wrong line". Several railwaymen are overseeing the operation. (R.Harrison)

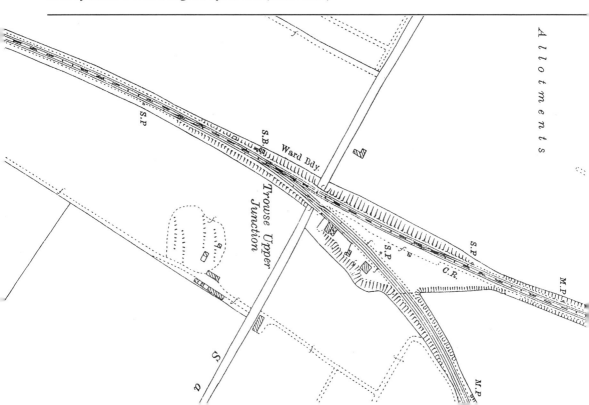

69. A total of 112 steam locomotives are known to have been cut up at King's scrapyard between February 1963 and February 1968. These included locomotives from all four pre-nationalisation companies, as well as a few BR standard designs. Amongst the earliest arrivals was County class 4-6-0 no. 1007 *County of Brecknock*, which reached the yard in mid-October 1963 and by 9th November the scrapping process was well advanced. (R.Harrison)

70. The scrapyard cranes tower over class U1 2-6-0s nos 31894, which still appears to have a tender full of coal, and 31896, as they await the torch in company with class K 2-6-0 no. 32337 on 25th April 1964. In the foreground are a number of coach underframes, which had probably lost their bodywork and fittings at the work site on the Ashwellthorpe line before being dragged here for final destruction. (R.Harrison)

71. The last steam engines arrived for scrapping in early 1968 but the yard continued to cut up rolling stock, as well as a handful of diesel locomotives, until it was closed in 1981. There is a thin layer of snow on the ground as King's shunter, formerly BR no. D2956, busies itself with wagons in the scrapyard sidings on 26th November 1969. (R.J.Adderson)

72. Industrial premises are very much in evidence to the west of the line as we look towards the junction on 3rd May 1982. No. 40013 passes the signal box at the top of the climb from Trowse with a special train returning to London, and an 80mph speed restriction sign confirms that the tortuous exit from Norwich is over, and that high speed running can now begin. (D.C.Pearce)

73. This six-arch viaduct carries the line from Diss over the meandering River Tas and the Norwich to Ely railway line. A class 90 electric locomotive propels a train from London over the viaduct on 28th February 2008, and the housing and Cattle Market site give the first indications to passengers that they are approaching Norwich. (M.Page)

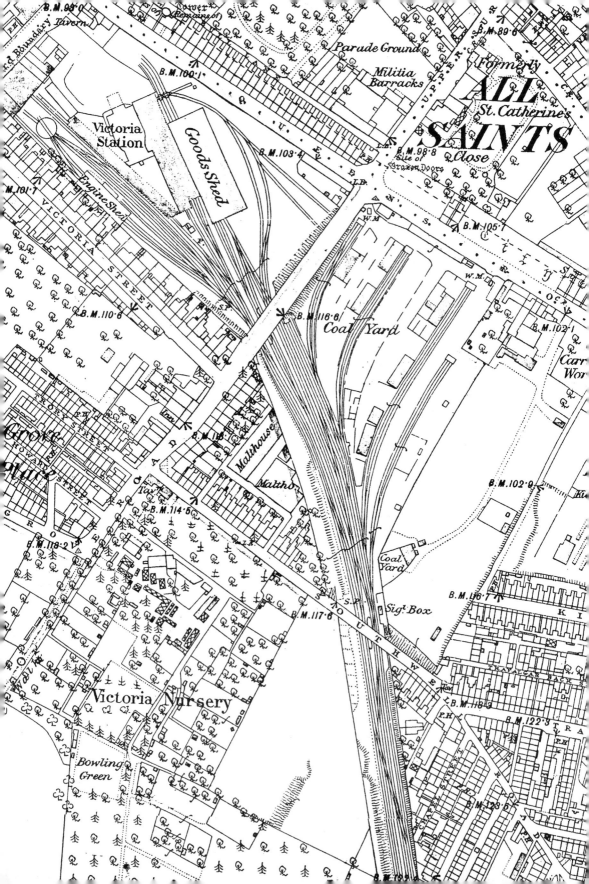

NORWICH VICTORIA

← XI. This 1886 map shows the site approaching its maximum extent. The main addition to the facilities was the use of the triangular area of land to the east of the Victoria Nursery for the expansion of coal yard capacity in 1901/03, at a cost approaching £5000. Road access was via a steep slope from Southwell Road. The engine shed was demolished and the turntable removed soon after the closure of the station to passenger services on 22nd May 1916. The following views will illustrate the route geographically rather than chronologically.

74. Late in the line's history, industrial development in the area around the junction brought additional rail traffic for a few years. Indeed, two new private sidings were installed in the first few hundred yards along the branch for the use of Robert Stevenson and Messrs Barnes & Pye in 1958 and 1963, respectively. With Stevensons engineering works in the background, an 0-6-0 diesel shunter stands on the already overgrown Barnes & Pye siding during the early 1970s. The sidings did not survive the decade, but the points leading to them remained in the running line until the end. (I.C.Allen/Transport Treasury)

75. A similar diesel locomotive brings up the rear of a long goods train as it runs between the back gardens on its way to Victoria, on a sunny day around 1960. The shunter had been at the front of the train from Trowse with the train engine at the back, but after reversal at Upper Junction, class B1 4-6-0 no. 61045 is leading once more. (I.C.Allen/Transport Treasury)

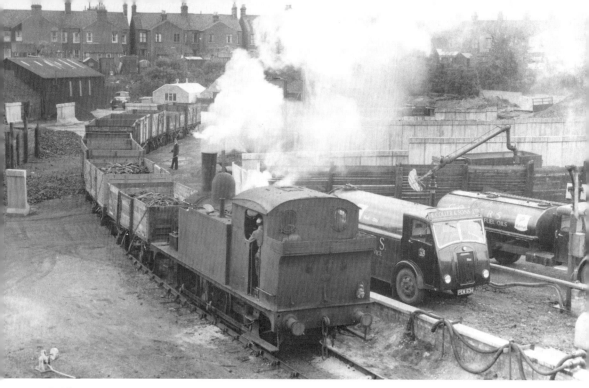

76. Class J69 0-6-0T no. 68555 is busy in the cramped Southwell Road yard, a group of six sidings which had been installed on a triangle of land to the south-west of the running lines early in the 20th century. It is 11th May 1957 and traffic appears to be thriving. (B.Harrison)

77. No. 08250 has arrived with loaded coal wagons on 13th June 1985 and is positioning them for unloading. To the right, the area once occupied by Southwell Road sidings is no longer rail-served and is now home to all manner of discarded industrial material, including the cab of an old Bedford lorry. (R.J.Adderson)

78. Another ex-GER 0-6-0T, class J67 no. 68516, runs past a line of wagons during the late 1950s. The extensive yards curve away in the distance towards Queens Road, with coal and cement traffic very much in evidence. A coal concentration depot was established on the site of these sidings in the late 1960s. (I.C.Allen /Transport Treasury)

79. The mechanised coal depot, fed by a conveyor belt from the railway, has changed the scene entirely on 4th August 1984. No. D2325, seen on the left, had arrived here in 1968, and was used to place the wagons over the coal drop for unloading. Although in National Coal Board ownership, the engine retained its BR number. Following the closure of the line in October 1986, a supermarket and car park were built on this site. (S.McNae)

80. During the final years, class 08s normally hauled the trains to the coal concentration depot from Thorpe station yard, but no. 31424 was negotiating the overgrown tracks on 24th June 1986. By the end of the century, most of the trackbed had been converted into a cycle way and footpath, with the bridges and cuttings providing lasting reminders of its former railway use. (R.J.Adderson)

UPPER JUNCTION. Messrs. Robert Stevenson's Siding and Messrs. Barnes & Pye Siding. These sidings are situated on the Down side of the line between Trowse Upper Junction and Norwich Victoria and are controlled by separate 1-lever ground frames. An Annett's Key which will release either ground frame is kept in Trowse Upper Junction signal box. The person in charge of a train calling at the siding(s) must obtain the key and return it to the signal box as soon as possible after the work at the siding is completed.

From *Sectional Appendix*, dated 1969.

81. Here is the frontage of the station itself, as it was in the early 20th century. The running lines headed off at different angles as they approached the platforms and as a result the building stood between the arrival and departure lines. The awnings seen on each side of the offices illustrate this unusual feature. (P.Standley coll.)

82. Looking towards the buffer stops, the area looks somewhat neglected in 1933, some 17 years after passenger services were withdrawn. However, both platforms and their canopies remain, and the track layout is much the same as it had been. The two tracks between the goods shed and the right hand awning are exposed to the elements although the map shows that they had been covered over in earlier years. (LOSA)

83. A few railtours were the only passenger trains known to have visited the branch to Victoria in the years after the passenger closure. The first of these took place on 8th September 1956, when a Norfolk Railway Society special called in the course of a trip covering a number of 'goods only' lines. Surrounded by enthusiasts, class E4 2-4-0 no. 62797 awaits departure time in the shadow of Southwell Road bridge. (NRS Archive)

Sunday School excursion, dated 2nd July 1903.

Norwich Victoria to Hethersett and back.
(New City Sunday School—about 500, Third Class).

				210 p.m.					211 p.m.	
Norwich Victoria	...	...	dep.	1 30	Wymondham	...	...	dep.	9 10	Cars
Trowse { Upper Junction	...	{ arr.	1 34	Hethersett	...	...	{ arr.	9 20	
		{ dep.	1 39				{ dep.	9 25	
{ Lower Junction	...	{ arr.	1 41	Trowse { Lower Junction	...	{ arr.	9 35	
		{ dep.	1 46			{ dep.	9 40	
†Hethersett	...	...	{ arr.	1 55	{ Upper Junction	...	{ arr.	9 42	
		{ dep.	1 58	Cars			{ dep.	9 47	
Wymondham	...	...	arr.	2 7	†Norwich Victoria	...	...	arr.	9 52	

84. The station buildings and platforms remained in place for nearly 37 years after the passenger services had ceased, and were eventually demolished in February 1953. A contemporary newspaper reported that a scheme for improvements to the goods yard had been brought forward owing to an urgent need for rubble to repair flood damage. The new work included the provision of a large area of concrete hard standing for road vehicles, and some alterations to the track layout. This was the busy scene in the late 1950s, looking northwards from Grove Road bridge. During the 12-week period to October 1958 some 23,255 tons of freight were handled here, but the goods yard was closed in January 1966 and the area has since been redeveloped. (R.J.Adderson coll.)

GREAT EASTERN RAILWAY
Issued subject to Regulations in the Company's Time Tables
NORWICH VICTORIA to
Norwich Vic   Norwich Vic
TIVETSHALL
Tivetshall   Tivetshall
1s 1½d   Fare   1s 1½d
Third Class

0186 9810

2nd- DAY DAY -2nd
EXCURSION EXCURSION
8 September 1956   8 September 1956
(S.T. K1629)   (S.T. K1629)
Norfolk Railway   Norfolk Railway
Society   Society
Eye to   Norwich
NORWICH   (Thorpe) to
(Thorpe)   EYE
Via Tivetshall &   Via Norwich (Victoria)
Beccles   & Tivetsh—l
                      (E)
For conditions see over   For conditio   over

0032 0032

TROWSE

Trowse Lower Junction & Trowse station

XII. The connecting line from Trowse
Upper Junction was opened as a single line in
1851 despite the Parliamentary Act's authority
for double track. The opening of the second
track did not take place until 1879. Until the
swing bridge over the River Wensum was
ready for traffic into Norwich Thorpe, this
station acted as the terminus for services
for a short period in 1845 when the line
from Ely first opened. It was one of
a number of stations that closed
soon after the start of WWII on
5th September 1939. The
map indicates
the situation
in 1907.

Lodge

S.P

Sheep Pens

S.P

S.B.

Sheep Pens

Cattle Pens

P.H.

Station

Boat
Houses

Tank

Tank

Sewage
(Norwich C

*TROWSE
MILLGATE*

S.R.

B.M.15·6

Boat
House

B.P

P.O.

P.H.

F.B.

S.R.H.W.M.O.T.

St. Andrew's Ch.

B.M.9

Highest Point to
which Ordinary
Tides flow

Boat Ho.

(Vicarage)

S.B.

Trowse Mill
S.P   *(Corn)*

F.B.

G.Yd.

Parish

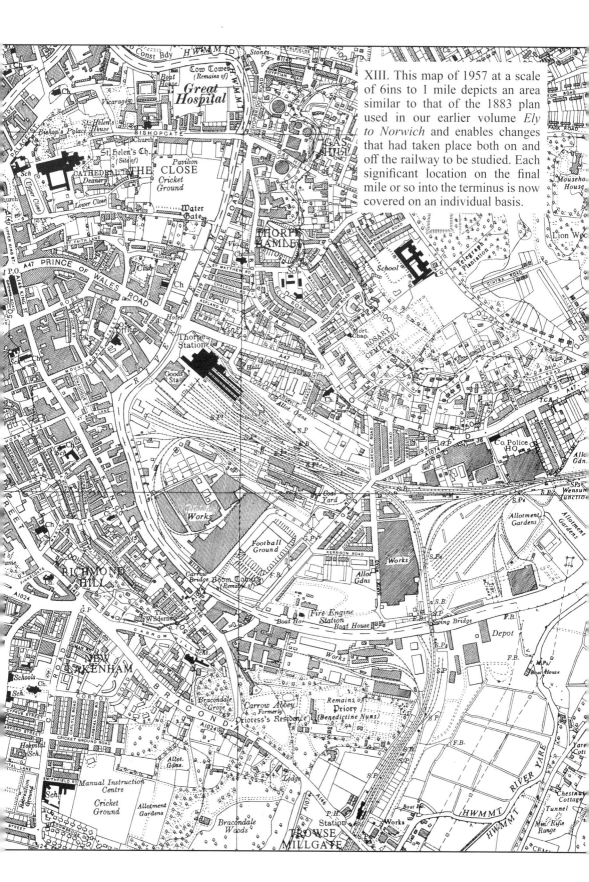

XIII. This map of 1957 at a scale of 6ins to 1 mile depicts an area similar to that of the 1883 plan used in our earlier volume *Ely to Norwich* and enables changes that had taken place both on and off the railway to be studied. Each significant location on the final mile or so into the terminus is now covered on an individual basis.

85. Class B1 4-6-0 no. 1235 is only a year or so old as it steams through Trowse station on 26th September 1948 with the 2.35pm train from Norwich Thorpe. It is scheduled to call at all stations between there and Ipswich. Passenger services had been withdrawn in 1939 as a temporary measure on the outbreak of war and, as things turned out, they were never restored. However, at this time the platforms, lighting, footbridge and awning remained, ready for a possible reopening. (E.Tuddenham/M&GN Circle)

> **For other views of Trowse, see Middleton Press album,** *Ely to Norwich.*

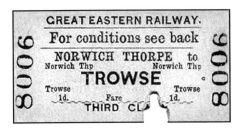

86. As a passenger train heads towards Norwich, 0-6-0T no. 68597 brings a long goods train through the platforms in September 1953. The lamps and waiting shelter are still in place on the up platform. For some years, the station saw occasional use for football traffic – on 3rd January 1953, for example, the 12.30pm local train from Ipswich was booked to make a special stop for the benefit of football supporters. (R.Harrison)

87. With a tender full of what appears to be fairly low quality coal, a class J15 0-6-0 propels a short goods train up the bank during the 1950s. In the distance, the track curves sharply round to Trowse Upper Junction, where the train will reverse and take the former main line into Victoria station. Whilst this was common practice, longer trains were operated with an engine at each end to simplify the reversal procedure. (I.C.Allen/Transport Treasury)

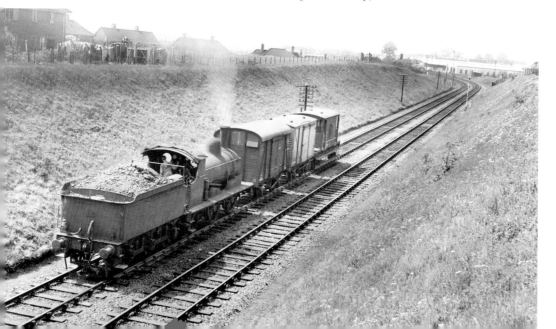

88. No. D202 climbs the 1 in 84 gradient towards Trowse Upper Junction with the 4.20pm relief train from Norwich Thorpe to Liverpool Street on Whit Monday, 18th May 1959. At that time BR still had the resources and capacity to provide additional trains on busy days. (B.Harrison)

89. Located in the angle of the lines to Ely and to Ipswich, Trowse Lower Junction signal box overlooks a line of condemned steam locomotives awaiting their final journey to the scrapyard on 18th April 1964. For two or three years, such line-ups were a frequent sight here in Victoria sidings, to the north of the Ipswich line. Class N1 2-6-0 no. 31822 is nearest the camera; then come two ex-GWR engines, 0-6-0 no. 2246 and 2-8-0T no. 5205, while the trio shown in picture 70 are at the far end of the line. Identification of the former GWR locomotives could sometimes be difficult, as their number plates had been removed and replaced with crudely painted, or worse, chalked, numerals fading away on the cabsides. (R.Harrison)

90. This is the signalman's view of the junction, looking towards Norwich on 29th June 1985. No. 47585 *County of Cambridgeshire* curves away from the Ely line with an up express, and the driver is applying power for the climb to Trowse Upper Junction. (R.J.Adderson)

91. The station saw a new lease of life at various times during 1986 when Norwich station was closed for remodelling work. Easter saw the greatest activity, when three platforms were in use to handle the trains diverted here. This was the scene in the forecourt on 29th March, with passengers boarding one of the buses which provided a shuttle service to and from Norwich station. Mail traffic was also dealt with, as the Post Office van beyond the building testifies. (R.J.Adderson)

92. The up platform was demolished during August 1987, but the down platform and buildings were still in place on 5th March 1999. A class 86 propels a train from London on the last stage of its journey, passing two class 37s as they prepare to attack the bank up to Trowse Upper Junction with a condensate train from North Walsham to Harwich. This traffic flow continued into 2018, providing the only regular freight traffic between on the line between Norwich and Diss. The area to the east of the station is occupied by a busy aggregates terminal, and a train of empty wagons occupies the loop line. (R.J.Adderson)

93. Having set out from Norwich Thorpe at 11.40am, the up 'East Anglian' express approaches the platforms on 5th September 1949. There are cattle pens on each side of the railway, and in the distance an 0-6-0 tank engine stands next to Trowse Yard signal box. All the coaches are Gresley designs painted in the new BR livery, whilst the engine, class B1 4-6-0 no. 61041, carries its new number although the tender is still lettered LNER. (E.Tuddenham/M&GN Circle)

94. No. 47487 curves round from the swing bridge and approaches the former station with a train for Liverpool Street on 19th June 1986. It is passing Trowse Yard signal box, which has already lost its nameboard, and was abolished on 29th November 1986. This was one of five signal boxes which survived until the late 1980s to control trains between Trowse Lower Junction and Norwich station, a distance of just over one mile. (R.J.Adderson)

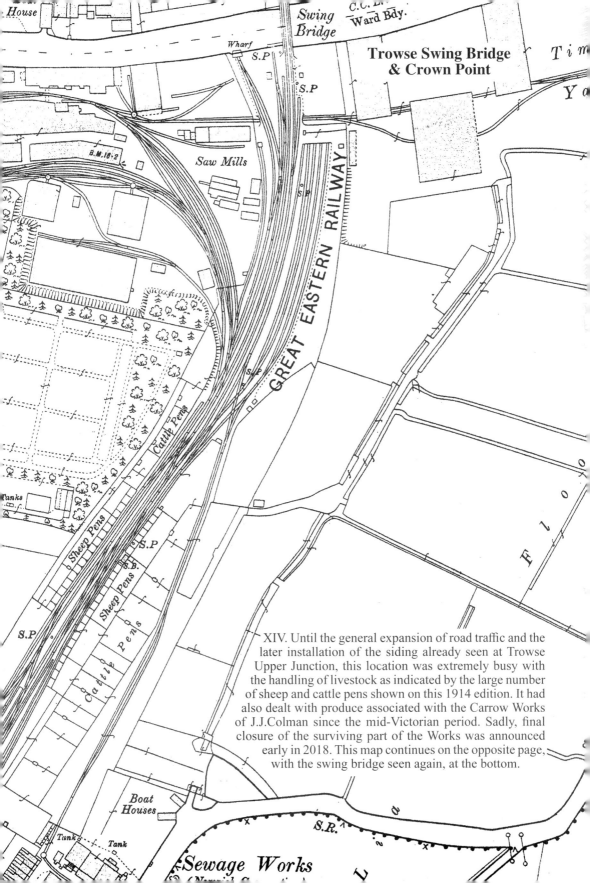

House

Swing
Bridge

Wharf

S.P

S.P

C.C.L
Ward Bdy.

**Trowse Swing Bridge
& Crown Point**

T i m

Y a

B.M.16·2

Saw Mills

S.P

GREAT EASTERN RAILWAY

S.P

Tanks

Cattle Pens

F l o o

Sheep Pens

S.P

S.B.

Sheep Pens

F

Cattle Pens

S.P

XIV. Until the general expansion of road traffic and the
later installation of the siding already seen at Trowse
Upper Junction, this location was extremely busy with
the handling of livestock as indicated by the large number
of sheep and cattle pens shown on this 1914 edition. It had
also dealt with produce associated with the Carrow Works
of J.J.Colman since the mid-Victorian period. Sadly, final
closure of the surviving part of the Works was announced
early in 2018. This map continues on the opposite page,
with the swing bridge seen again, at the bottom.

*Boat
Houses*

Tank

Tank

S.R.

a

L

Sewage Works

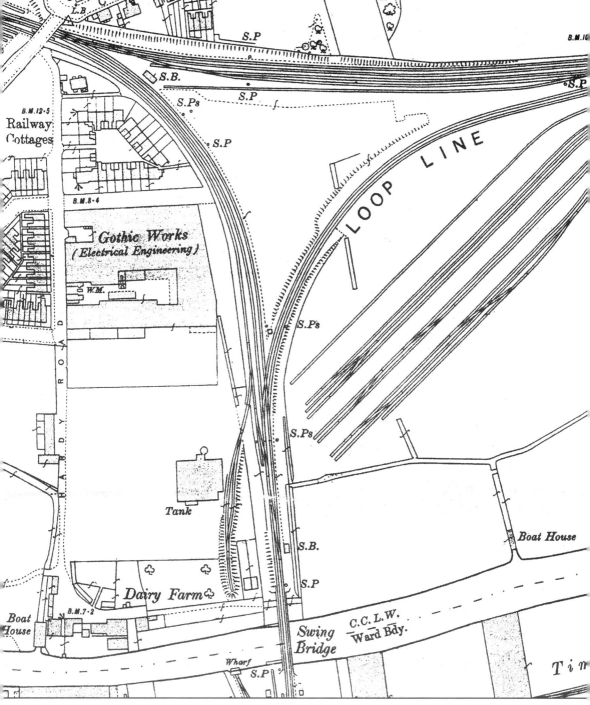

XV. There have been three such structures crossing the River Wensum at this point. As shown on this 1914 map, the 1845 single track bridge was replaced in 1906 by one with a double track using the original centre pivot. This was, in turn, superseded by a more modern example, albeit with just a single track, in connection with electrification in January/February 1987. The new bridge was constructed to the west of the 1906 structure, but the original 1845 centre pivot remained in place although obscured by scrub and undergrowth. The network of sidings shown to the north-east of the bridge was installed to handle traffic for the 1911 Royal Agricultural Show, held on the Crown Point estate to the south of the river. This name was adopted for the new maintenance depot, which was opened in September 1982. The route into the terminal station via Thorpe Junction is indicated in the north-west corner of the map.

95. The GER went to considerable trouble to provide additional facilities in connection with the 1911 Agricultural Show. Two temporary platforms were provided on the avoiding line, and four more on the land to the south of this, catering not only for passengers but also for livestock and materials bound for the showground. This was the scene on 29th June, with the curved through platforms to the right and much activity in the terminal platforms at a slightly lower level. (GERS/Windwood coll.)

96. This unusual view shows the 1906 bridge being swung to enable shipping to pass. We are looking roughly north-eastwards through the girders on 4th April 1959, and the wooden structure on the left of the bridge contains the operating equipment. A gasometer and the city's power station dominate the background. (R.Harrison)

97. A very clean class K3 2-6-0, no. 61970 from Lowestoft shed, is about to cross the River Wensum as it passes Trowse Swing Bridge Junction signal box with a lengthy up goods train on Saturday 4th April 1959. (R.Harrison)

98. A large yard was built on the site of the 1911 temporary platforms and is seen here around 1970, with class 37 and 03 diesel locomotives going about their business. This view is looking in a westerly direction, and the lines to the swing bridge run between the sidings and the range of buildings in the distance. (G.L.Kenworthy coll.)

➔ 99. During the early 1980s, the yard area was chosen for the establishment of a new maintenance facility for locomotives and rolling stock. This was long overdue, as diesel locomotives were still using the old steam shed buildings, while coaches were being serviced in the open air at Great Yarmouth. Here we see the early stages of the construction work, with a line of ballast wagons standing on the avoiding line, and a variety of stock in the Engineer's sidings beyond. (G.L.Kenworthy coll.)

100. The replacement swing bridge, carrying just a single line, was brought into use on 15th February 1987 and some three months later, on 29th May, no. 86244 *The Royal British Legion* brings an up train across the river. A fixed overhead bar on the swinging span, connecting with the catenary at each end of the bridge, carries the electric current, and this arrangement is clearly visible. (R.J.Adderson)

➔ 101. Crown Point Traction Maintenance depot became operational in October 1982. We are looking southwards on 27th August 2017, with the swing bridge at the top centre of the picture and the lines to the coast in the foreground. No fewer than seven of Greater Anglia's fleet of class 90 locomotives appear in this picture. (M.Page)

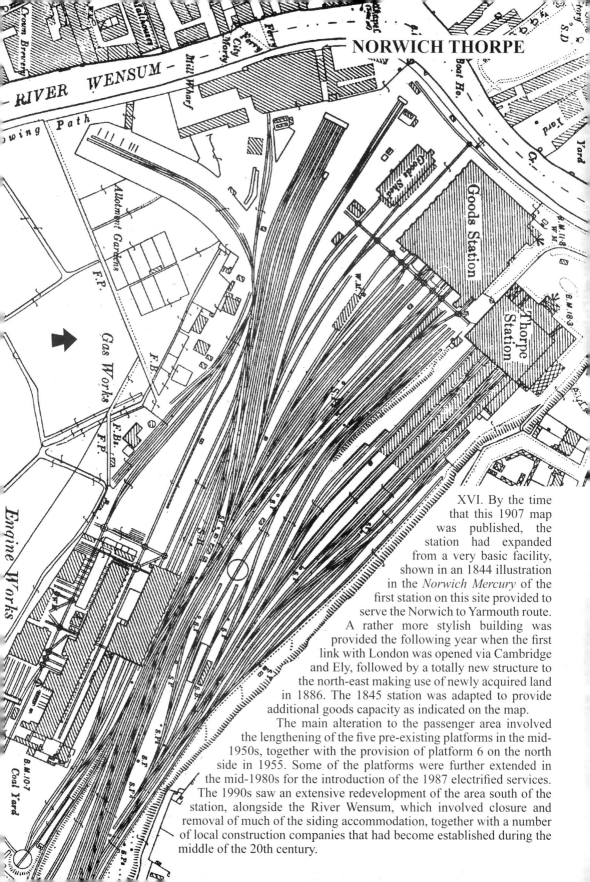

XVI. By the time that this 1907 map was published, the station had expanded from a very basic facility, shown in an 1844 illustration in the *Norwich Mercury* of the first station on this site provided to serve the Norwich to Yarmouth route. A rather more stylish building was provided the following year when the first link with London was opened via Cambridge and Ely, followed by a totally new structure to the north-east making use of newly acquired land in 1886. The 1845 station was adapted to provide additional goods capacity as indicated on the map.

The main alteration to the passenger area involved the lengthening of the five pre-existing platforms in the mid-1950s, together with the provision of platform 6 on the north side in 1955. Some of the platforms were further extended in the mid-1980s for the introduction of the 1987 electrified services.

The 1990s saw an extensive redevelopment of the area south of the station, alongside the River Wensum, which involved closure and removal of much of the siding accommodation, together with a number of local construction companies that had become established during the middle of the 20th century.

102. We start our coverage with six photographs showing the station, yards and locomotive shed as they were in October 1911, and here the bridge carrying Carrow Road provides a fine panoramic view of the station approaches. The lines curving away under the signal gantry lead to the 1886 station, whilst those continuing straight ahead give access to the original 1844 passenger station, by now used only for goods traffic. Sidings to the left of the goods lines are packed with wagons loaded with locomotive coal, and beyond them a dozen or more engines are standing outside the shed. A number of horse boxes are amongst the wagons in the siding to the right of the picture. (GERS/Windwood coll.)

103. Now we move to the passenger signal box, for a view of the deserted station platforms. Again, there is a horsebox standing in the carriage sidings on the right, while the only sign of life is provided by a locomotive shunting coaches in the sidings. This photograph is dated 8th October 1911, which was a Sunday, and no doubt accounts for the lack of activity. (GERS/Windwood coll.)

104. Once more there is an uncharacteristic stillness to the scene as we look towards the four road engine shed on the same day. The shed building itself is thought to date back to the 1840s, as did the range of single-storey offices and the works beyond. (GERS/Windwood coll.)

105. The photographer's vantage point for our previous picture was at the lower end of the inclined track to the coal drops on which the wagons are standing. Here we are looking eastwards, with the houses on Carrow Road in the distance. There is coal everywhere, in wagons, in locomotive tenders, in stacks and in piles on the ground. (GERS/Windwood coll.)

106. Now we are now looking in the opposite direction, with the unmistakable dome of the passenger station to the right, together with carriage sidings and one of the two locomotive turntables. The original station is behind the three signal posts in the centre, whilst wagons occupy most of the extensive sidings beyond the Goods Yard signal box.
(GERS/Windwood coll.)

107. Our final 1911 view is again eastwards, with the distant Carrow Road bridge spanning the tracks beyond the signal gantry. The carriage sidings and goods sidings are full of stock, while the massive bulk of the locomotive shed dominates the right background. (GERS/Windwood coll.)

G. E. R.

Norwich (Thp.)

G. E. R.

From_____

TO

NORWICH
          THORPE

108. The inaugural 'East Anglian' express leaves for Liverpool Street on 27th September 1937. Introduced with much publicity, this train and the down working were scheduled to link Norwich and the capital in an unprecedented 135 minutes, inclusive of a stop at Ipswich. The engine, class B17/4 4-6-0 no. 2859 *East Anglian*, was one of two which had been renamed and fitted with streamlined casing for use on this prestigious service, whilst the coaches were new and built specially for the train. (R.J.Adderson coll.)

109. The LNER era saw much-needed investment and improvements, not least of which was the provision in 1936 of a mechanical coaling plant at the locomotive shed. This structure, still fairly new, overlooks a quartet of 4-4-0s in the shed yard. Whilst it was no longer necessary to shovel coal laboriously from wagon to tender, other work remained dirty and backbreaking, as the chap on the right, faced with piles of ash to load into the wagon, would no doubt testify. (RCTS)

From *Good Lines*, monthly journal of the Temperance Society, dated 1911.

110. In addition to the turntable seen in picture 106, there was another one next to Carrow Road, and scenes like this were freely available to passers-by. No wonder it was a favourite location for a generation of trainspotters in the 1950s! Here, a railwayman strains to turn a B1 4-6-0, whilst class WD 2-8-0 no. 90191 takes water in the shed yard. Completing the scene, 'Britannia' class 4-6-2 no. 70040 *Clive of India* stands alongside the coaling tower. (M.Fordham)

111. Class B1 4-6-0 no. 61109 sets out with an up express on 10th May 1953, passing class J39 0-6-0 no. 64726, which is waiting on an engineers train. The track layout has not altered greatly compared with that seen in picture 102, but the signalling has been simplified considerably. (R.Harrison)

112. The platforms and sidings are full of rolling stock as we look westwards across the station area during the late 1950s. At least three diesel multiple units mingle with an array of coaches of both BR and LNER designs. (R.J.Adderson coll.)

113. 'Britannia' class 4-6-2 no. 70006 *Robert Burns* has arrived at platform 4 with an express from Liverpool Street on 17th May 1958. By this time, DMUs had taken over most of the local services in the area, but, despite the influx of main line diesels from 1957, steam locomotives were rostered to some of the London expresses until September 1961. (M.Fordham)

114. The concourse of the station reveals a host of once-familiar details on 31st March 1962. The Empire tobacconists and W.H.Smith stalls are prominent, whilst a number of automatic vending machines are dotted around – notably that encircling the pillar in the centre of the picture. Blue enamel signs abound, pointing out the various facilities available, and these indicate that hungry visitors had the choice of either 'Refreshments' or 'Dining and Tea Room'. Part of the train departure indicator appears next to the bookstall, while Moss Bros and the local ITV station vie for attention on the walls. (B.D.J.Walsh/GERS)

115. As we can see from the map, a line curved round from the back of the yard to the appropriately named Riverside Works, home of Boulton & Paul, the well-known engineering firm. Their office block is in the background as the company's Baguley diesel shunter moves a load of steel around the site on 14th January 1983. We are looking northwards along Riverside, and the track of a long-disused siding to the quayside emerges from the mud in the foreground. (R.J.Adderson)

116. No. 47580 *County of Essex* sets out with the 11.25am to Liverpool Street on 8th November 1983. The semaphore signals and complex trackwork provide a traditional setting, which would be swept away within a couple of years. (J.R.Sides)

117. On 27th July 1985, no. 47467 stands behind the large signal box which controlled movements in the station area. Whilst the fleet of class 47s based at Stratford handled the vast majority of the London trains at this time, locos from other depots made occasional appearances. Of these, no. 47467 was almost certainly the furthest from home, being allocated to Inverness shed. The rebuilt Goods Yard signal box is in the middle distance, and railway tracks still occupy all the land between the station and the river. (R.J.Adderson)

118. The full electric service began on 11th May 1987, but there were occasional instances of service trains being electrically hauled before then. The 8.25am from Liverpool Street on 28th April is thought to be the first such working, and a celebratory photo shoot took place to mark the occasion before no. 86253 *The Manchester Guardian* headed the train back to London. (G.L.Kenworthy)

119. The class 86 electric locos maintained the electric services into the new century, but were gradually replaced by newer class 90s from 2002 onwards. No. 86238 *European Community* retains the Anglia Railways colours as it waits at the platform on 1st April 2004. Behind it, no. 90003 *Raedwald of East Anglia* has been painted in the 'One' livery to mark the start of the new franchise that day. (R.J.Adderson)

120. Now bearing National Express livery, no. 90003 gathers speed as it leaves the platforms with a London express on 28th May 2010. The locomotive is at very much the same point as that in picture 116, but the track layout has altered considerably since the pre-electrification remodelling of the area, and the overhead equipment has transformed the scene. (R.J.Adderson)

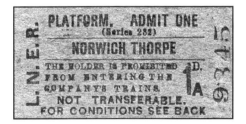

For other views of Norwich, see *Ely to Norwich*, *Branch Lines around Wroxham*, *South Lynn to Norwich City*, *Branch Lines East of Norwich* and *Norwich Tramways*.

MP Middleton Press

EVOLVING THE ULTIMATE RAIL ENCYCLOPEDIA

Easebourne Midhurst GU29 9AZ. Tel:01730 813169

www.middletonpress.co.uk   email:info@middletonpress.co.uk

A-978 0 906520   B- 978 1 873793   C- 978 1 901706   D-978 1 904474
E - 978 1 906008   F - 978 1 908174   G - 978 1 910356

96